BLACK-CAPPED CHICKADEE *(Parus atricapillus).* Found year-round in northern half of U.S. and western Canada.

EASTERN BLUEBIRD *(Sialia sialis)*. Summer: southeastern Canada, northeastern and north central U.S. Year-round: southeastern and south central U.S.

Fifty Favorite Birds
Coloring Book

Lisa Bonforte

About This Book

The fifty different birds illustrated in this book are commonly occurring examples of species seen in or near cities and towns in most parts of the United States (not including Hawaii) and Canada. Please note that the birds shown are adult males unless otherwise specified.

Artist Lisa Bonforte has based her drawings on the paintings by Bob Hines in *Fifty Birds of Town and City*, a booklet published in 1978 by the U.S. Department of the Interior Fish and Wildlife Service (editors: Bob Hines and Peter A. Anastasi). In addition to these beautiful, ready-to-color pictures, Ms. Bonforte has provided color versions at the back of the book as a guide for identification and accurate coloring.

In the present volume, the captions give the common and scientific names of the birds as well as the seasons and ranges in which they occur in the United States and Canada.

LEFT: WHITE-BREASTED NUTHATCH *(Sitta carolinensis)*. Year-round through most of U.S. RIGHT: BROWN CREEPER *(Certhia familiaris)*. Summer: southern and western Canada, northern U.S. Winter: eastern two-thirds of U.S. (excluding northernmost states). Year-round: western U.S. and parts of Northeast.

BROWN THRASHER *(Toxostoma rufum)*. Summer: northeastern and
north central U.S. Year-round: southeastern U.S.

CANADA GOOSE *(Branta canadensis)*. Winter: southern and western
U.S. Migrant throughout U.S. in spring and fall.

CARDINAL *(Richmondena cardinalis)*. Female left, male right. Year-round in most parts of the U.S.

CATBIRD (*Dumetella carolinensis*). Summer: most of U.S. except West
Coast. Winter: extreme southeastern U.S.

CEDAR WAXWING *(Bombycilla cedrorum)*. Male left, female right. Summer: southern Canada and far northern U.S. Winter: southern half of U.S. Year-round: northeastern and north central U.S.

CHIMNEY SWIFT *(Chaetura pelagica)*. Found in summer in eastern half of U.S.

CHIPPING SPARROW (*Spizella passerina*). Summer: most of Canada and U.S. Year-round: southeastern and southwestern U.S.

COWBIRD (Eastern Cowbird; Brown-headed Cowbird; *Molothrus ater*).
Female left, male right. Summer: western Canada and northern half of U.S.
Year-round: most of southern half of U.S.

COMMON CROW *(Corvus brachyrhynchos)*. Summer: most of Canada.
Year-round: most of U.S.

DOWNY WOODPECKER *(Dendrocopus pubescens)*. Female left, male right. Year-round in most of U.S. and wooded parts of Canada.

FLICKER *(Colaptes auratus)*. Summer: most of Canada. Year-round: generally, eastern half of U.S.

GREEN HERON (*Butorides virescens*). Found in summer in eastern half of U.S.

HERRING GULL (*Larus argentatus*). Summer: Canadian far north. Winter: North American coasts. Migrant throughout U.S. and Canada.

HOUSE SPARROW *(Passer domesticus)*. Male left, others female. Year-round throughout U.S. and southern Canada.

HOUSE WREN (*Troglodytes aedon*). Summer: most of U.S. Winter: Gulf Coast and part of southwestern U.S.

SLATE-COLORED JUNCO *(Junco hyemalis)*. Male in foreground, female in background. Summer: most of Canada. Winter: most of U.S.

ABOVE: KILLDEER *(Charadrius vociferus)*. Summer: southern Canada and northern U.S. Year-round: southern U.S. **BELOW: MALLARD** *(Anas platyrhynchos)*. Female in foreground, male in background. Summer: most of Canada. Winter: most of U.S.

MOCKINGBIRD *(Mimus polyglottos)*. Year-round in most of U.S. except
northwestern and north central states.

MOURNING DOVE (*Zenaidura macroura*). Year-round in most of U.S.

MYRTLE WARBLER *(Dendroica coronata)*. Male above, female below.
Summer: most of Canada. Winter: generally, southern U.S. Found as
migrant in most of U.S.

BELOW: NIGHTHAWK (*Chordeiles minor*). Found in summer throughout U.S. and Canada. ABOVE: TURKEY VULTURE (*Cathartes aura*). Summer: northern U.S. Year-round: southern U.S.

PIGEON *(Columba livia)*. Year-round throughout U.S. and in much of
Canada.

PURPLE MARTIN *(Progne subis)*. Found in summer in most of U.S.

RED-EYED VIREO *(Vireo olivaceus)*. Found in summer in much of
Canada and most of U.S. (not Southwest).

RED-HEADED WOODPECKER *(Melanerpes erythrocephalus)*. Summer:
north central U.S. Year-round: most of eastern U.S.

SPARROW HAWK (*Falco sparverius*). Summer: most of Canada, northern U.S. Year-round: southern U.S. and West Coast.

STARLING *(Sturnus vulgaris)*. Summer: southern Canada. Year-round: throughout U.S.

TOWHEE *(Pipilo erythrophthalmus)*. Male above, female below. Found in most of the U.S. most of the year.

TUFTED TITMOUSE *(Parus bicolor)*. Found year-round in eastern half of the U.S.

SONG SPARROW *(Melospiza melodia)*. Summer: most of Canada. Winter:
southern U.S. Year-round: northern U.S.

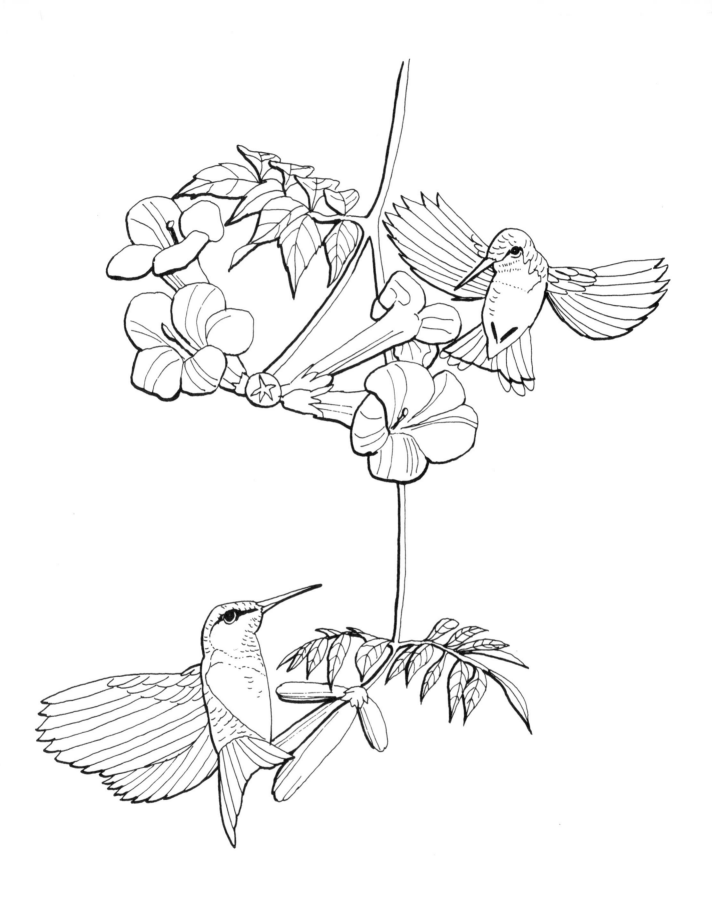

RUBY-THROATED HUMMINGBIRD (*Archilochus colubris*). Male left, female right. Found in summer in eastern half of U.S.

WHITE-CROWNED SPARROW *(Zonotrichia leucophrys)*. Summer: northern and western Canada. Winter: southern U.S. Year-round: U.S. West Coast and west central states. Migrant in eastern Canada and northeastern U.S.

EASTERN WOOD PEWEE *(Contopus virens)*. Found in summer in eastern half of U.S. and parts of southeastern Canada.

YELLOWTHROAT *(Geothlypis trichas)*. Male above, female below. Summer: most of Canada and U.S. Year-round: southernmost states of U.S.

YELLOW WARBLER *(Dendroica petechia)*. Found in summer in most of Canada and U.S.

BUTTERFLIES
Coloring Book

Jan Sovak

Captions by Monty Reid

About This Book

Butterflies are the most notable exception to the many unpleasant pictures that come to mind when one thinks about insects. As far as most people are concerned, butterflies are simply exquisite. And, although some caterpillars (the caterpillar being the first, or larval, stage in the life of a butterfly) can actually be seriously destructive to forests and farms, the sight of a butterfly's delicate and colorful beauty begs forgiveness.

One or another of the world's 20,000 or so species of butterflies may be found almost everywhere on all continents except Antarctica. About 700 species have been identified in North America north of Mexico. Artist Jan Sovak has drawn 43 of these lovely creatures for this coloring book; including drawings of the only two butterfly species native to Hawaii. Writer Monty Reid has added informative captions to the drawings. Mr. Sovak has also provided small color versions of his drawings that can be found at the back of this book. Use them for inspiration as you color each illustration or as an accurate nature identification guide on a summer afternoon.

The common and scientific names follow Robert Michael Pyle, *The Audubon Society Field Guide to North American Butterflies* (New York: Knopf, 1981), as does the order of the drawings. With one exception, this order is taxonomic (that is, based on considerations of anatomy and evolution). The exception involves the Skippers. The Skippers are actually an entirely separate group, or "superfamily," of Lepidoptera (order of butterflies, moths and their allies) sharing some characteristics of moths as well as of butterflies. These are traditionally classified before true butterflies, but, as they are less familiar to most people, Pyle places them at the end, as we do here.

Phoebus Parnassian (*Parnassius phoebus*). Bright red spots decorate the pale wings of the Phoebus Parnassian. Its antennae are short and usually ringed with black-and-white markings. This member of the family of Swallowtails and Parnassians (over 600 species worldwide) is found high in the mountains from California to Alaska. It is, especially for a butterfly, unusually well adapted to the cold, sometimes active even in snowstorms.

51

Pipevine Swallowtail *(Battus philenor).* Orange, blue and white markings on its underwings help identify the Pipevine Swallowtail. It lays its rust-colored eggs on pipevines and related plants, upon which the caterpillar feeds when it emerges. As with Monarch butterflies and milkweed, the pipevines contain a substance that gives Pipevine Swallowtails an unpleasant flavor to birds. The adults feed on a broad variety of plants. Found in most of the United States, as well as Mexico.

Tiger Swallowtail *(Pterourus glaucus)*. Brilliant yellow-and-black wings and teardrop-shaped "tails" are characteristic of this very large butterfly (wingspan to over 5 inches), although some females have dark brown wings trimmed with blue markings. West of the Rockies and south of Canada the Tiger Swallowtail is replaced by the similar Western Tiger Swallowtail. Both are among the most common and conspicuous butterflies in North America.

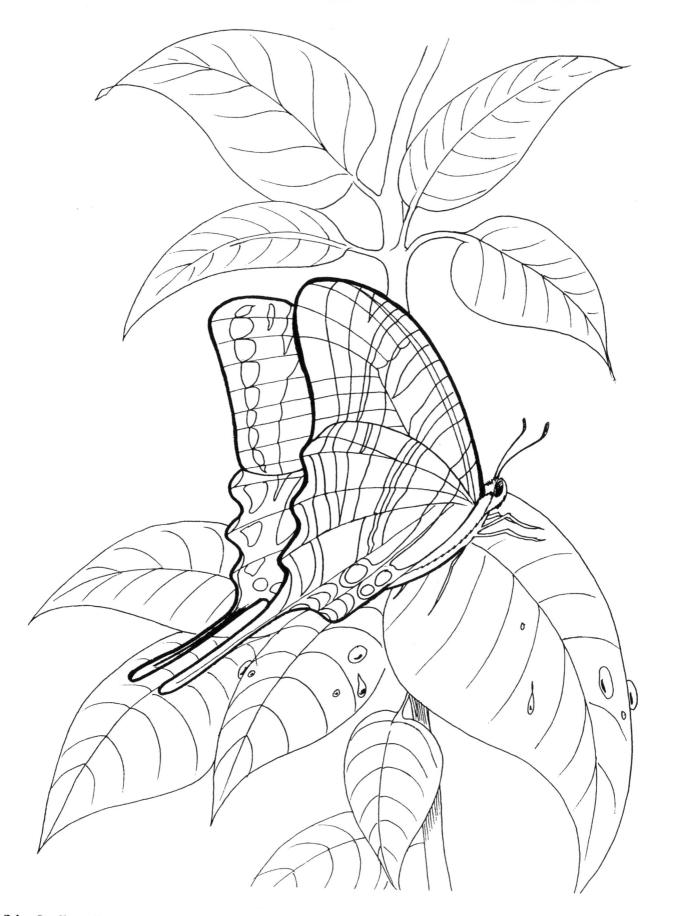

Zebra Swallowtail (*Eurytides marcellus*). Bright red spots at the bottom of its large triangular wings and similarly colored streaks and spots underneath, and its swordlike ''tail,'' make the Zebra Swallowtail easy to identify. If you look closely you will see that the antennae are rusty red as well. Found throughout much of eastern North America, but only where there are pawpaw trees or their relatives.

54

Sara Orangetip *(Anthocharis sara)*. This butterfly (a member of the family of Whites and Sulphurs, with about 1,000 species worldwide) can be found along the western coast of North America, from Baja California up to Alaska. Its forewings have bright orange tips but its underwings are a mottled green with yellow patches. Like many butterflies, Sara Orangetips live for only a few weeks.

Dogface Butterfly (*Zerene cesonia*). Dogface Butterflies are often seen tacking over fields of clover, a favorite food source. Wing markings seem to form the profile of a poodle, hence the name Dogface. An agile, rapid flier, this member of the family of Whites and Sulphurs is most common in the southern United States but sometimes may be found as far north as Canada.

56

California Dogface (*Zerene eurydice*). The state insect of California, this spectacular butterfly can be found on mountainsides and in forest clearings. Males (bottom) have mustard-colored hind wings, with a black-bordered dogface-shaped patch on the forewings that often takes on a rich plum hue. Females (top) are a pale yellow, with only the slightest hint of the border.

Orange-barred Giant Sulphur (*Phoebis philea*). The bright yellow with brilliant orange markings on the upperwings of the male (females are similar but less brilliant) makes this one of the most striking of the Sulphurs. While the caterpillars of the Orange-barred

Giant Sulphur live only on sennas, the adult may take nectar from any number of plants, using its long tongue, or proboscis. This powerful flier is primarily a tropical butterfly. The only sizable population in the United States is in south Florida.

59

Harvester *(Feniseca tarquinius).* This slow-flying butterfly with orange-and-black wings can usually be found in moist areas throughout much of North America, but especially the East. Like all members of the enormous Gossamer Wing family (some 7,000 species worldwide, including the Coppers, Hairstreaks and Blues), it holds its wings over its back when resting. One of the most unusual butterflies, its caterpillar eats only aphids. The adult feeds on aphid honeydew, from which food supply it rarely strays far.

Ruddy Copper *(Chalceria rubidus)*. The color of burnished copper, this butterfly has dark speckles, and sometimes white tips, on its wings. The Ruddy Copper is a fast flier and a familiar sight in the hot sun of high meadows in the West. The caterpillars feed largely on wild rhubarb, while the adults prefer flowers of cinquefoil, rabbit brush and wild buckwheat.

61

Colorado Hairstreak *(Hypaurotis crysalus).* Found in the canyons and scrublands of the Southwest, the Colorado Hairstreak has deep purple wings, generally with golden-orange spots. The tiny hairlike projections on its hind wings are characteristic of the Hairstreaks. Unlike most butterflies, the Colorado Hairstreak may remain active even after sunset.

Great Purple Hairstreak *(Atlides halesus)*. Living primarily in the Southern half of the United States, the Great Purple Hairstreak is found only in association with mistletoes. The male, really more blue than purple, is brighter than the female, which, however, has more prominent "tails" on its wings.

Olive Hairstreak *(Mitoura gryneus)*. The Olive Hairstreak has a dark brown back (females may have orange or gold over the brown) with some orange-brown or golden-brown. Underneath, both sexes look entirely different, showing bright green with prominent white lines. This Hairstreak, unlike most, is common in the East, found, however, only around Eastern Red Cedar and related trees.

64

Blackburn's Bluet *(Vaga blackburnii)*. One of only two species of butterflies native to the Hawaiian Islands, the lovely Blackburn's Bluet (the female is blue and black; the male has more extensive blue) remains common in many habitats. It feeds on the Hawaiian koa tree and certain other native and introduced plants.

65

Orange-bordered Blue *(Lycaeides melissa).* It is the female that gives the name to this striking butterfly, where bright orange margins on the upperwings contrast with a bluish gray-brown wing base. Fairly common in open spaces of the West and far Midwest, from Canada to Mexico, the Orange-bordered Blue is also found in small numbers in isolated colonies in the eastern Midwest and East. The northeastern subspecies was named "Karner Blue" by novelist Vladimir Nabokov, who was also a distinguished lepidopterist (butterfly specialist).

Common Blue (*Icaricia icarioides*). This small, pale blue butterfly can be seen in the early spring in most parts of North America. Females are mostly brown, making them less prominent so they remain hidden from birds and other predators. The caterpillars live on lupine plants. They secrete a sweet liquid known as honeydew, which usually attracts ants. The ants in turn offer protection from some of the caterpillars' predators.

Little Metalmark (*Calephelis virginiensis*). The male (bottom) of this tiny species (about as big as your thumbnail!) has slightly bolder markings than the female. Both are mostly orange, with silver-green markings. Little Metalmarks may often be seen resting on thistle leaves with wings outspread, looking like tiny rust spots. (Unlike many other butterflies, Metalmarks, a separate family of about 1,000 species worldwide, do not fold their wings over their backs when resting.)

Gulf Fritillary (*Agraulis vanillae*). The Brush-footed Butterflies, to which family the Gulf Fritillary belongs, is a large one, encompassing about 3,000 species worldwide. This beautiful bright orange member of the also-large subgroup of Fritillaries is found primarily in the South, particularly around the Gulf of Mexico. It frequently invades the North without success, unable to tolerate the winters. (Brush-footed Butterflies continue from here through page 89.)

Julia *(Dryas iulia)*. Another striking orange Brush-footed Butterfly, the Julia, like the Gulf Fritillary, feeds on passion flowers in the American South. Going a step further, however, the caterpillar of the Julia chooses poisonous species, making the adult distasteful to preda-tors. In addition, it is more strictly subtropical, being found only in the extreme southern parts of Florida and Texas. Also, like all the Brush-footed Butterflies, the Julia has stunted forelegs, on which it cannot walk.

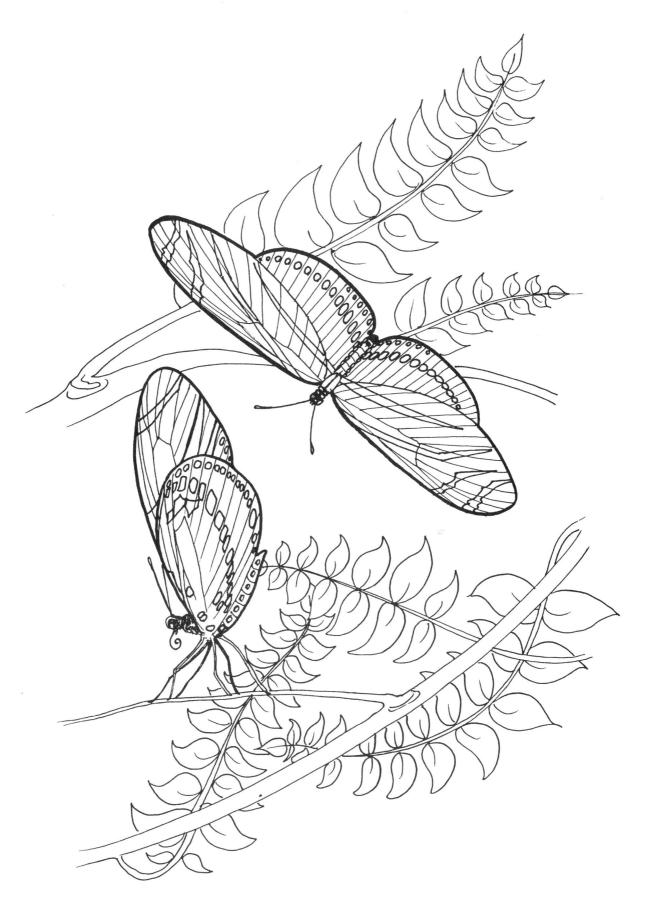

Zebra Longwing *(Heliconius charitonius).* Slow but dignified, the Zebra Longwing is a weak flier. Long antennae and a slender body are typical of these butterflies, which are at home in the tropics but can sometimes be found as far north as Kansas. The Zebra Longwing is a long-lived butterfly (which means that it lives for several months, most butterflies surviving only a few weeks), but its brilliant black-and-yellow markings attract the attention of many predators.

Diana *(Speyeria diana)*. Diana was an ancient goddess who lived in the woods. This beautiful butterfly does too. It can be found along woodland streams in much of the South and Midwest, but is common only in parts of the Great Smoky Mountains. The male is black and orange, with a spangle of silver on its hind wings. The female (top

left) is black and iridescent blue, with pale blue spots on its forewings. The Diana belongs to the group of Fritillaries, a subgroup of the Brush-footed Butterflies. Unfortunately the widespread cutting of forests has decreased the range of the Diana.

Chalcedon Checkerspot *(Euphydryas chalcedona)*. Most common in California, this medium-size black, orange and cream-colored Brush-footed butterfly is found in a variety of habitats in the far West, from southwest Oregon to Nevada, Arizona and Mexico. The drawing also shows the chrysalis (left), the intermediate stage between caterpillar and adult butterfly. Chrysalises, hung from a plant with a bit of silk, are unlike the cocoon of a moth, which is wrapped entirely in silk.

Question Mark (*Polygonia interrogationis*). A silvery question mark on the underside of its mottled hind wings gives this member of the Anglewing group of the Brush-footed Butterflies its name. The edges of its wings look ragged and often have a purple hue. Able to lay its eggs in any number of trees, particularly elms, the Question Mark is able to thrive in many places east of the Rocky Mountains, from Canada to Mexico. The adults frequently feed on fermented fruit, leading sometimes to the butter-flies' becoming intoxicated!

75

Mourning Cloak *(Nymphalis antiopa).* When its dark wings are folded, a Mourning Cloak resting on dark bark is perfectly camouflaged. When its wings are open, however, blue-and-yellow trim on a dark maroon-brown background highlights a distinctively beautiful and widely distributed butterfly. Found everywhere in North America except where it is very dry or cold. Look for them especially near trees in the willow, poplar and elm families.

Milbert's Tortoiseshell (*Aglais milberti*). A close relative of the Mourning Cloak, Milbert's Tortoiseshell prefers the cool temperatures of northern latitudes (it is absent from Alaska, however); it may also be found further south in alpine meadows. Its dark coloration is typical of butter- flies of cooler climates, dark tones absorbing heat from the sun more readily than lighter tones. The dark areas of its two-toned wings thus help to regulate the Milbert's Tortoiseshell's body temperature.

Painted Lady *(Vanessa cardui)*. Bearing distinctive wings of black, salmon-orange and white with blue spots, the Painted Lady is found throughout North America, Europe, Asia and Africa, even Iceland, where there are few kinds of butterflies. It is absent from colder regions in winter, but recolonizes them by late spring, making it one of the most widespread of all butterflies. Its favorite plant is thistle.

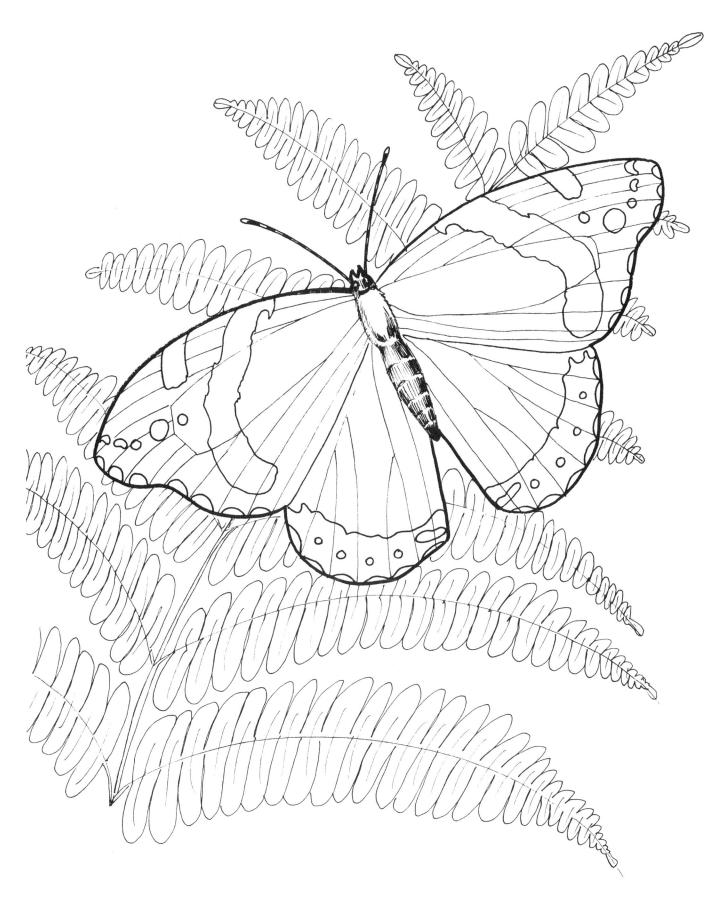

Red Admiral *(Vanessa atalanta)*. The swift-flying Red Admiral, with brilliant red or orange bars across its wings, can be found throughout the warmer parts of North America year-round; in spring it migrates north as well, making it one of the most widespread of butterflies. Quiet in full sunshine, Red Admirals can often be seen courting at dusk. Courtship is an elaborate ritual that includes the dusting of the female with special scent scales that function as an aphrodisiac.

Kamehameha *(Vanessa tameamea)*. Closely related to the Red Admiral but with a distinctive coloration of its own, the Kamehameha was named after a Hawaiian king. It is confined to the Hawaiian islands, where it is common, and is one of only two species of butterflies native to Hawaii (Blackburn's Bluet is the other). The caterpillars feed on mamake and other plants in the nettle family. Adults are often found in koa woods and vegetated clearings.

Buckeye *(Junonia coenia).* The black eyespots on this butterfly are trimmed with yellow and have iridescent blue centers that make them seem like holes through which the sky is peeping. In summer, Buckeyes may be found in open areas throughout much of North America. In the fall, they migrate south, in some areas in massive numbers.

81

Malachite *(Siproeta stelenes)*. The large black-and-jade Malachite is one of the most impressively beautiful of North American butterflies, although its color tends to fade after exposure to bright sunlight. Unfortunately it is essentially a tropical species and may be seen only in Texas and southern Florida.

82

White Admiral *(Basilarchia arthemis)*. White Admirals are often seen flitting along the edges of forests in New England, where they lay their eggs on willows, poplars and birches. They are found elsewhere as well, but only in the North, from southeast Alaska to British Columbia and from Manitoba through New York. The prominent white band across the White Admiral's mostly coal-black wings makes it easy to identify. Because its wings often have a purple iridescence, some people call this butterfly the Banded Purple.

Red-spotted Purple *(Basilarchia astyanax).* Butterfly wings are covered with tiny overlapping scales, creating fascinating color patterns as well as the kind of iridescence for which the Red-spotted Purple is famous. On top, this butterfly's wings show a rich blue-green iridescence; underneath, they look entirely different, with prominent orange-red spots. The Red-spotted Purple's range extends in a very rough triangle from New England to Arizona to Florida, including parts of Colorado and the Dakotas.

Lorquin's Admiral *(Basilarchia lorquini)*. This strictly Western species shows wavy spotted cream-colored bands across its brownish black fore and hind wings, which are also tipped with buff or orange. Lorquin's Admiral is among the most aggressive of butterflies, readily harassing birds immensely larger than itself. It was named for the nineteenth-century French collector Pierre Lorquin.

85

California Sister (*Adelpha bredowii*). Another Western butterfly, the California Sister got its name from its wings' resemblance to a nun's habit. The resemblance ends, however, with its bright red-orange wingtips and the orange, brown and lavender of its underwings. Especially common in California, the California Sister is found particularly in forests of live oak, the main host plant of the caterpillars. The adults are often found drinking spilled wine at wineries.

Blue Wing (*Myscelia ethusa*). The brilliant sapphire-blue of its upperwings makes this poorly known butterfly distinctive in North America. It is only marginally North American, however, being essentially a tropical species that just barely makes it up into southern Texas. Its underwings are a drab brown and gray, good camouflage colors that protect it from predators when it rests with closed wings.

87

Ruddy Daggerwing (*Marpesia petreus*). The ragged edges and daggerlike "tails" of this brilliantly colored orange-and-black butterfly are said to frighten off predators. This is another tropical species the northern limit of whose range is in Florida and Texas. In Florida the caterpillars feed on leaves of fig and cashew trees. Adults will feed on rotting figs, as well as other fruits and giant milkweed.

Pavon (*Doxocopa pavon*). The Pavon is yet another tropical member of the huge Brush-footed Butterfly family that just barely enters the United States, in southeast Texas, and even there only rarely. The bright purplish shine of the males' upperwings is apparent only in bright sunlight.

Canada Arctic *(Oeneis macounii).* This yellowish-brown and brown butterfly lives up to its name, thriving even in the southern part of Canada's Northwest Territories and making it into the United States only in northern Minnesota and a small part of Michigan. The caterpillars take two years to mature, and adults are seen only in alternate years. For some reason they appear only in odd years west of Lake Winnipeg, Manitoba, and only in even years east of that point! This is the only representative in this book of the very large family of Satyrs (about 3,000 species worldwide).

Monarch *(Danaus plexippus)*. Among the best-known butterflies in North America, Monarchs can be seen around milkweeds when breeding and in many different habitats across the continent at other times. They are the long-distance champions among migrating butterflies, some covering thousands of miles. Far Western Monarchs overwinter in southern California, but Eastern and Mid-western Monarchs fly all the way to the middle of Mexico each fall. Unlike migrating birds, however, no individual makes a complete round-trip; on the northward journey in the spring they breed and are replaced by their offspring for the remainder of the trip. Finally, on their northern-most breeding grounds, a new brood is produced, which in fall gathers in huge swarms for the trip south.

Queen *(Danaus gilippus)*. Along with the Monarch one of the very few North American members of the Milkweed Butterfly family (about 300 species worldwide), the Queen is another large, beautiful butterfly, with rich orange-brown, dark-veined coloration. It is, however, far less widely distributed than the Monarch, ranging through the South up as far as Nevada, Kansas and Georgia. The caterpillars, like those of all Milkweed Butterflies (and a number of other species as well), feed on milkweed, which contains a toxin that is retained in the adults and makes these butterflies distasteful to birds.

Arizona Skipper (*Codatractus arizonensis*). With the Skippers we come to a very different group of butterflies, more closely related to the moths than the others in this book (with about 3,000 species worldwide, the Skippers are placed in a "superfamily" of their own). Many are very tiny and drab-colored. The Arizona Skipper is large for a Skipper (up to about 2¼ inches across, while some Skippers are only ½ inch) and shows some tawny-brown and purplish coloring on its otherwise dark brown wings. It is found only in certain arid parts of the Southwestern United States, as well as Mexico. Although it is not rare, its breeding cycle is poorly known.

93

Long-tailed Skipper (*Urbanus proteus*). Widespread in the South, the Long-tailed Skipper often migrates as far north as Connecticut. Distinguished by a lovely green iridescence on its back, this large, mothlike Skipper is unfortunately destructive to many crops. The caterpillars particularly favor bean plants.

Fiery Skipper (*Hylephila phyleus*). Of a more typical size for a Skipper (about an inch across), the Fiery Skipper is mostly a bright yellow-orange. The caterpillars feed on many plants in the grass family, including sugarcane. Not surprisingly, the Fiery Skipper is most common in the South, including the Southwest, but it is sometimes found as far north as Michigan and Connecticut.

AMERICAN
WILD FLOWERS
Coloring Book

Rendered for coloring by

Paul E. Kennedy

──── About This Book ────

The wild flowers in this book have been drawn by Paul E. Kennedy from the paintings of individual plants prepared by Mary Vaux Walcott and published by the Smithsonian Institution in 1925. They have long been recognized as exceptionally fine renderings. Seven additional paintings by Dorothy Falcon Platt (pages 100, 101, 105, 113, 121, 131, 140) have been redrawn through the courtesy of Crown Publishers, Inc.

These flowers have been selected from the large Walcott and Platt collections to show the breadth of beauty of American wild flowers. Favorites and frequently met flowers have been preferred, with a few unusual items that are specially suited for coloring.

Most of the plants shown are widely spread through the eastern half of the United States, with several that are almost national. A few striking plants from the West have also been included. Scientific names correspond to those in *Gray's Manual of Botany*, plus occasionally other authorities. Common names reflect local usage, and may vary from area to area.

The originals, numbered to correspond to the pages of the book, have been reproduced in exact color in the back of the book. This color and identification guide will assist you in creating realistic images as well as help you to accurately identify many important wild flowers and their close relatives.

Balsam-root *(Balsamorhiza sagittata)*. West Coast

Bee-balm *(Monarda didyma)*. East, Midwest

Black-eyed Susan *(Rudbeckia hirta)*. East, Midwest

Blue Phlox *(Phlox divaricata)*. East, Midwest

Bluebells, Virginia Cowslip *(Mertensia virginica)*. East, Midwest

Bottle-gentian (*Gentiana saponaria*). East, Midwest

Buttercup *(Ranunculus acris)*. Naturalized from Europe. East, Midwest

California-Poppy *(Eschscholtzia californica)*. West Coast

Cardinal-flower (*Lobelia cardinalis*). East, Midwest

Cobra-plant, California pitcher-plant *(Darlingtonia californica)*. West Coast

Columbine *(Aquilegia canadensis)*. East, Midwest

Cow-lily (*Nuphar advena*). East, Midwest

Early Azalea (*Rhododendron roseum*). East

Flame-Azalea *(Rhododendron-calendulaceum).* East

Goldenrod (*Solidago* species). East, Midwest

Great Laurel, Rosebay *(Rhododendron maximum)*. East

Green-banded Mariposa *(Calochortus macrocarpus)*. West Coast

Harebell, Bluebell (*Campanula rotundifolia*). Widely spread

Indian Paint-Brush *(Castilleja miniata)*. West, similar species in East

Jack-in-the-pulpit, Indian-Turnip (*Arisaema atrorubens*). East

Marsh-marigold, Cowslip *(Caltha palustris)*. Widely spread

Mountain-laurel *(Kalmia latifolia)*. East, Midwest

New England Aster *(Aster novae-angliae)*. East, Midwest

Pasque-flower *(Anemone patens)*. West, Midwest

Passion-flower *(Passiflora incarnata)*. South, Midwest

Pitcher-plant (*Sarracenia purpurea*). East, Midwest

Prickly Pear (*Opuntia* species). Southwest, similar forms elsewhere

Purple Pentstemon *(Pentstemon lyallii)*. West

Showy Lady's-slipper, Moccasin-flower *(Cypripedium reginae)*. East, Midwest

Small Purple Fringed Orchid *(Habenaria psycodes)*. East, Midwest

Spiderwort *(Tradescantia virginiana)*. East, Midwest

Swamp Iris, Blue Flag (*Iris versicolor*). East, Midwest

Swamp Mallow *(Hibiscus palustris)*. East

Tall Larkspur *(Delphinium elongatum)*. West

Trout Lily, Yellow Dogs-tooth Violet (*Erythronium americanum*). East

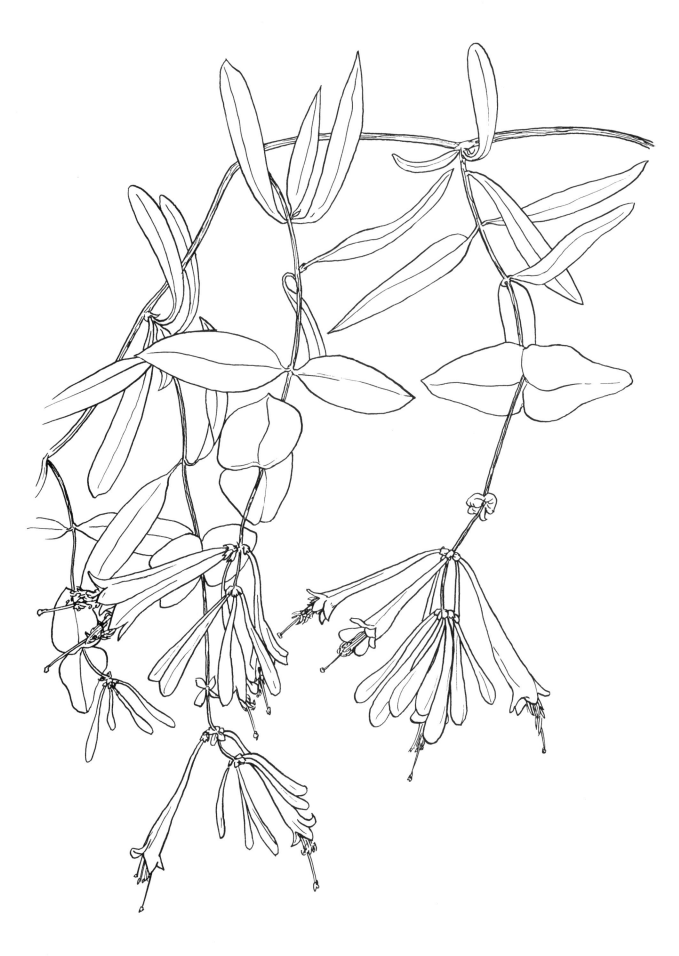

Trumpet-honeysuckle, Coral-honeysuckle *(Lonicera sempervirens)*. East, Midwest

Trumpet-vine, Cross-vine *(Bignonia capreolata)*. South, Midwest

Turk's-cap-lily *(Lilium superbum)*. East

Water-lily (*Nymphaea odorata*). Widely spread

Waxy-leaved thistle *(Cirsium undulatum)*. West

Western Red Lily *(Lilium philadelphicum andinum)*. West, similar forms in East

Wild Geranium *(Geranium maculatum)*. East, Midwest

Wild Lupine *(Lupinus perennis)*. East

Wild Pink *(Silene caroliniana)* Middle Atlantic states

Willowherb, Fireweed *(Epilobium angustifolium)*. Widely spread

Yellow jessamine *(Gelsemium sempervirens)*. South

Favorite Birds
Color and Identification Guide

Baltimore Oriole   (page 3)

Barn Swallow   (page 4)

Black-capped Chickadee   (page 5)

Eastern Bluebird   (page 6)

Blue Jay   (page 7)

Bobwhite   (page 8)

White-breasted Nuthatch &
Brown Creeper   (page 9)

Brown Thrasher   (page 10)

Canada Goose   (page 11)

Cardinal   (page 12)

Catbird   (page 13)

Cedar Waxwing   (page 14)

Chimney Swift   (page 15)

Chipping Sparrow   (page 16)

Cowbird   (page 17)

Common Crow   (page 18)   Downy Woodpecker   (page 19)   Flicker   (page 20)   Goldfinch   (page 21)

Grackle   (page 22)   Green Heron   (page 23)   Herring Gull   (page 24)   House Sparrow   (page 25)

House Wren   (page 26)   Slate-colored Junco   (page 27)   Killdeer & Mallard   (page 28)   Mockingbird   (page 29)

Mourning Dove   (page 30)   Myrtle Warbler   (page 31)   Nighthawk & Turkey Vulture (page 32)   Pigeon   (page 33)

Purple Martin   (page 34)

Red-eyed Vireo   (page 35)

Red-headed Woodpecker   (page 36)

Red-winged Blackbird   (page 37)

Robin & Wood Thrush   (page 38)

Ruby-throated Hummingbird
(page 39)

Song Sparrow   (page 40)

Sparrow Hawk   (page 41)

Starling   (page 42)

Towhee   (page 43)

Tufted Titmouse   (page 44)

White-crowned Sparrow   (page 45)

Eastern Wood Pewee   (page 46)

Yellowthroat   (page 47)

Yellow Warbler   (page 48)

Butterflies
Color and Identification Guide

Phoebus Parnassian   (page 51)

Pipevine Swallowtail   (page 52)

Tiger Swallowtail   (page 53)

Zebra Swallowtail   (page 54)

Sara Orangetip   (page 55)

Dogface Butterfly   (page 56)

California Dogface   (page 57)

Orange-barred Giant Sulphur   (pages 58 & 59)

Harvester   (page 60)

Ruddy Copper   (page 61)

Colorado Hairstreak   (page 62)

Great Purple Hairstreak   (page 63)

Olive Hairstreak   (page 64)

Blackburn's Bluet   (page 65)

Orange-bordered Blue   (page 66)

Common Blue   (page 67)

Little Metalmark   (page 68)

Gulf Fritillary   (page 69)

Julia   (page 70)

Zebra Longwing   (page 71)

Diana   (pages 72 & 73)

Chalcedon Checkerspot   (page 74)

Question Mark   (page 75)

Mourning Cloak   (page 76)

Milbert's Tortoiseshell   (page 77)

Painted Lady   (page 78)

Red Admiral   (page 79)

Kamehameha   (page 80)

Buckeye   (page 81)

Malachite   (page 82)

White Admiral   (page 83)

Red-spotted Purple   (page 84)

Lorquin's Admiral   (page 85)

California Sister   (page 86)

Blue Wing   (page 87)

Ruddy Daggerwing   (page 88)

Pavon   (page 89)

Canada Arctic   (page 90)

Monarch   (page 91)

Queen   (page 92)

Arizona Skipper   (page 93)

Long-tailed Skipper   (page 94)

Fiery Skipper   (page 95)

American Wild Flowers
Color and Identification Guide

Balsam-root   (page 99)

Bee-balm   (page 100)

Black-eyed Susan   (page 101)

Blue Phlox   (page 102)

Bluebells   (page 103)

Bottle-gentian   (page 104)

Buttercup   (page 105)

California-Poppy   (page 106)

Cardinal-flower   (page 107)

Cobra-plant   (page 108)

Columbine   (page 109)

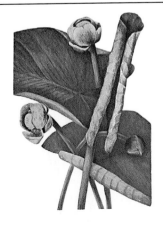

Cow-lily   (page 110)

Early Azalea   (page 111)

Flame-Azalea   (page 112)

Goldenrod   (page 113)

Great Laurel, Rosebay   (page 114)

Green-banded Mariposa   (page 115)

Harebell, Bluebell   (page 116)

Indian Paint-Brush   (page 117)

Jack-in-the-pulpit, Indian-Turnip
(page 118)

Marsh-marigold, Cowslip   (page 119)

Mountain-laurel   (page 120)

New England Aster   (page 121)

Pasque-flower   (page 122)

Passion-flower   (page 123)

Pitcher-plant   (page 124)

Prickly Pear   (page 125)

Purple Pentstemon   (page 126)

Showy Lady's-slipper,
Moccasin-flower   (page 127)

Small Purple Fringed Orchid
(page 128)

Spiderwort   (page 129)